Awesome Addition & Scary Subtraction

Paul Broadbent

In a hidden cave, far away in a magical land, lives a wise wizard, called Whimstaff. Every now and again, he searches for a young apprentice, so he can pass on his magical Maths powers. And this time, Whimstaff has chosen you!

Whimstaff shares the cave with a goblin and a little, red dragon. Pointy, the goblin, is very clever. The dragon, called Miss Snufflebeam, breathes small puffs of fire. She is clumsy and often loses the wizard's magical letters and numbers.

Pointy has two greedy, pet frogs, called Mugly and Bugly, who are very lazy and spend most of their time croaking, eating and sleeping. But every so often, they amaze Pointy by helping with an exercise!

Wizard Whimstaff and his friends are very happy in their cave, solving Maths problems. Join them on a magical quest to become a fully qualified Maths wizard!

Contents

Devilish Doubles

We're Mugly and Bugly and we're here to give you a brain cell alert! We have a magical method for **adding multiples of ten** that leaves us more time to snooze!

Once you know your doubles it's easy! Look at the pattern in these sums.

$9 + 9 = 18$
$90 + 90 = 180$
$900 + 900 = 1800$
$9000 + 9000 = 18\,000$

$15 + 15 = 30$
$150 + 150 = 300$
$1500 + 1500 = 3000$

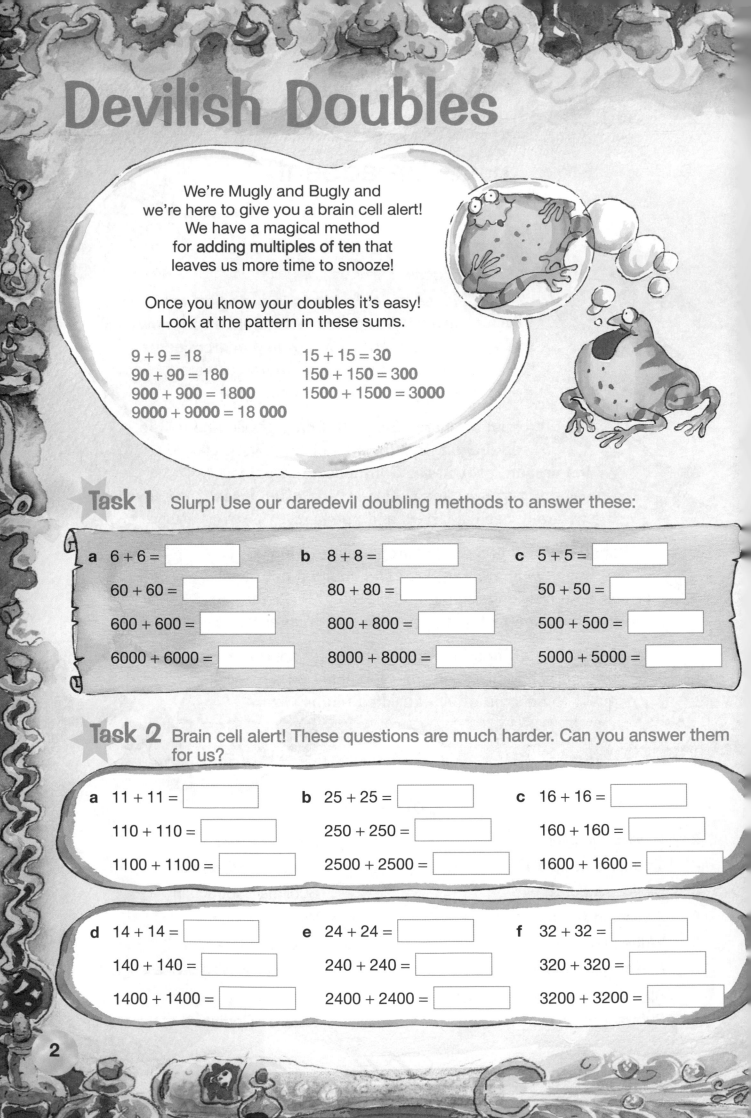

Task 1 Slurp! Use our daredevil doubling methods to answer these:

a $6 + 6 = $ ☐

$60 + 60 = $ ☐

$600 + 600 = $ ☐

$6000 + 6000 = $ ☐

b $8 + 8 = $ ☐

$80 + 80 = $ ☐

$800 + 800 = $ ☐

$8000 + 8000 = $ ☐

c $5 + 5 = $ ☐

$50 + 50 = $ ☐

$500 + 500 = $ ☐

$5000 + 5000 = $ ☐

Task 2 Brain cell alert! These questions are much harder. Can you answer them for us?

a $11 + 11 = $ ☐

$110 + 110 = $ ☐

$1100 + 1100 = $ ☐

b $25 + 25 = $ ☐

$250 + 250 = $ ☐

$2500 + 2500 = $ ☐

c $16 + 16 = $ ☐

$160 + 160 = $ ☐

$1600 + 1600 = $ ☐

d $14 + 14 = $ ☐

$140 + 140 = $ ☐

$1400 + 1400 = $ ☐

e $24 + 24 = $ ☐

$240 + 240 = $ ☐

$2400 + 2400 = $ ☐

f $32 + 32 = $ ☐

$320 + 320 = $ ☐

$3200 + 3200 = $ ☐

Task 3 Burp! Write the total amounts for each of these twin packs of magic ingredients.

a  HERBS 180g HERBS 180g Total _____ g

b 210 EYEBALLS 210 EYEBALLS Total _____ eyeballs

c STARDUST STARDUST Total _____ g

d 120 SPIDERS 120 SPIDERS Total _____ spiders

e NECTAR 1500ml NECTAR 1500ml Total _____ ml

Sorcerer's Skill Check

One last thing before we all have a snooze! Draw a line from each number to its double.

3200　　7000　　1600　　700　　350　　560

5000　　4200　　280　　2100　　14 000　　10 000

You can now add your gold star to your certificate, young apprentice! Super!

Troublesome Totals

Hello, I'm Wizard Whimstaff! To become a maths master wizard, like me, you must know the **number facts** for different totals.

Here are the **addition** facts for 9.

Now look at the **addition facts** for 900 and 9000.

9	900	9000
0 + 9	0 + 900	0 + 9000
1 + 8	100 + 800	1000 + 8000
2 + 7	200 + 700	2000 + 7000
3 + 6	300 + 600	3000 + 6000
4 + 5	400 + 500	4000 + 5000

What do you make of these **addition facts** for 9000?

100 + 8900   200 + 8800   4500 + 4500   6300 + 2700

Task 1 Some of the numbers on my magic scrolls have vanished! Help me by writing in the missing numbers.

a **The Complete Scroll of 400**

300 + _____

_____ + 200

100 + _____

b **The Answer is 700**

_____ + 200

400 + _____

600 + _____

c **It all adds up to 800**

500 + _____

_____ + 600

_____ + 400

Task 2 These secret sums make special spells. Write the missing number so each sum totals 500.

a 300 + _____   b _____ + 400   c 450 + _____

d 250 + _____   e _____ + 480   f _____ + 110

Task 3 Draw a line to join pairs of cauldrons that total 1000.

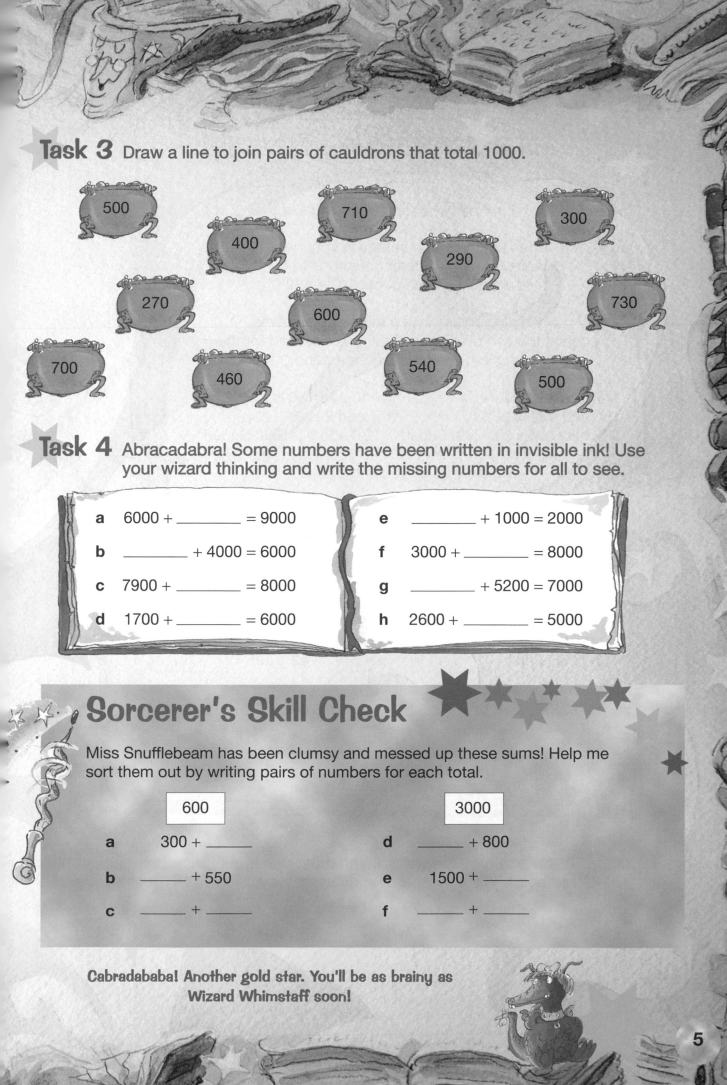

500
710
300
400
290
270
600
730
700
540
460
500

Task 4 Abracadabra! Some numbers have been written in invisible ink! Use your wizard thinking and write the missing numbers for all to see.

a 6000 + _____ = 9000

b _____ + 4000 = 6000

c 7900 + _____ = 8000

d 1700 + _____ = 6000

e _____ + 1000 = 2000

f 3000 + _____ = 8000

g _____ + 5200 = 7000

h 2600 + _____ = 5000

Sorcerer's Skill Check

Miss Snufflebeam has been clumsy and messed up these sums! Help me sort them out by writing pairs of numbers for each total.

600

a 300 + _____

b _____ + 550

c _____ + _____

3000

d _____ + 800

e 1500 + _____

f _____ + _____

Cabradababa! Another gold star. You'll be as brainy as
Wizard Whimstaff soon!

5

Mental Meddling

I'm Pointy, Wizard Whimstaff's
clever assistant!
When **adding two numbers** in your head,
there are many different methods to try.
How would you work out 147 + 132?

My magic spells have a mind of their own.
Look at the two different mental methods I did for this
addition when I waved my wand.

147 add 3 is 150   140 add 130 is 270
150 add 132 is 282   7 add 2 is 9
282 take away 3 is 279. Super!   270 add 9 is 279. Super!

It's easy when you know how!

Task 1 Practice makes perfect! So work these out in your head and write
the answers.

a 313 + 72 = [   ]   e 580 + 273 = [   ]

b 155 + 204 = [   ]   f   42 + 196 = [   ]

c 628 + 36 = [   ]   g 761 + 82 = [   ]

d 17 + 449 = [   ]   h 335 + 186 = [   ]

Task 2 To be a true maths wizard, you must use lots of different magic mental
methods. Work these out in different ways and write the answers.

a 273 + 37 = [   ]   b 638 + 112 = [   ]

c 94 + 678 = [   ]   d 456 + 297 = [   ]

Task 3

Help me find the answer to each sum and then use the code to find the names of 3 countries in Europe.

I	P	L	N	A	D	T	F	S	Y
602	519	161	790	483	546	926	374	855	237

a 546 + 56 = ☐ ____ **b** 240 + 615 = ☐ ____ **c** 163 + 211 = ☐ ____

792 + 134 = ☐ ____   25 + 494 = ☐ ____   513 + 89 = ☐ ____

79 + 404 = ☐ ____   364 + 119 = ☐ ____   607 + 183 = ☐ ____

74 + 87 = ☐ ____   565 + 37 = ☐ ____   76 + 85 = ☐ ____

148 + 89 = ☐ ____   238 + 552 = ☐ ____   274 + 209 = ☐ ____

395 + 395 = ☐ ____

19 + 527 = ☐ ____

Sorcerer's Skill Check

Write the correct total in each box. Super!

| 190 |
| 117 | 73 |
| 71 | 46 | 27 |

a
| 34 | 52 | 19 |

b
| 80 | 67 | 90 |

c
| 28 | 16 | 63 |

d
| 47 | 24 | 59 |

e
| 94 | 45 | 38 |

f
| 71 | 58 | 96 |

Slurp! Give yourself a gold star! Careful, if you get too clever, we might call you Pointy!

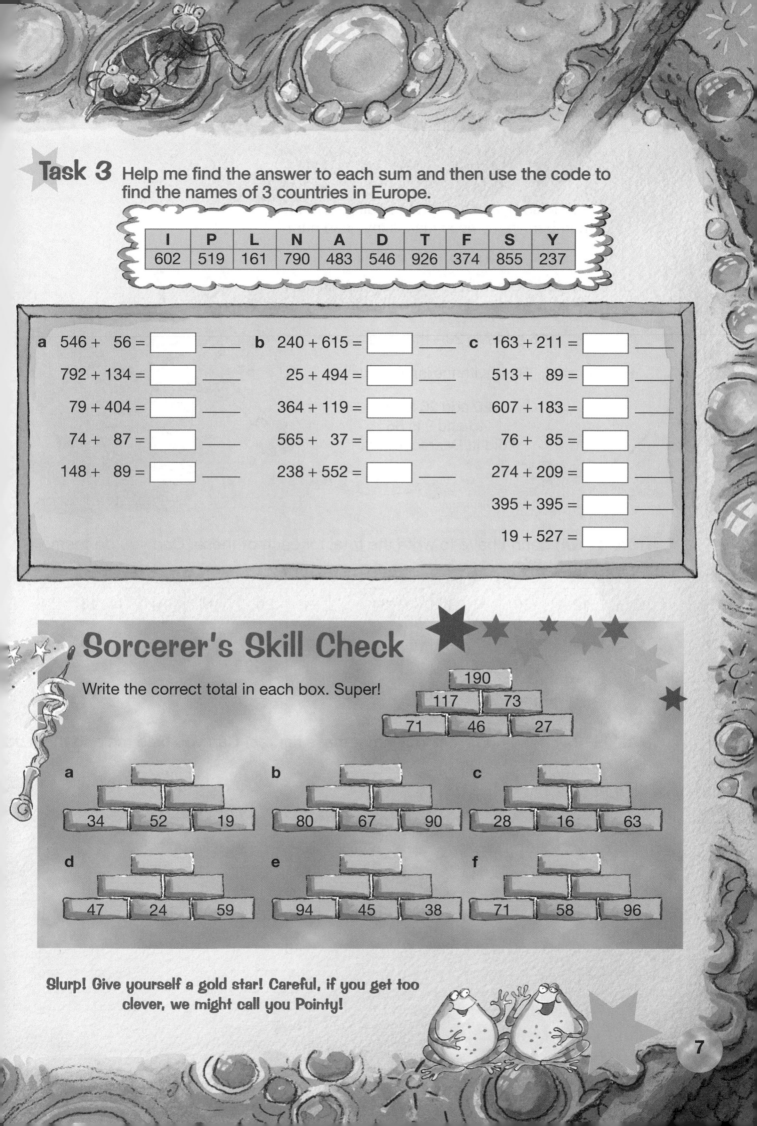

Awesome Adding

I'm Miss Snufflebeam and **adding several numbers** in my head makes my head hurt!

$$13 + 26 + 7 + 9 = ?$$

Oh dear! Can I remember what Wizard Whimstaff said? Yes! It was, "Look for pairs that are easy to add".

13 add 7 is 20 – that was easy!

He also said, "Start with the largest number."

20 add 26 is 46
46 add 9 is **55**
I did it! Dabracababra!

Task 1 Oh dear! I have to write the total for each of these. Can you do them for me?

a
12   30
23
= [ ]

b
34
21   69
= [ ]

c
26   14
7
= [ ]

d
18
25   12
= [ ]

Task 2 My head hurts just looking at these figures. Can you help me add them up

a
42   14
6   7
= [ ]

b
25   16
54   25
= [ ]

c
30   19
11   42
= [ ]

d
5   37
13   23
= [ ]

e
45   16
46   4
= [ ]

f
8   32
18   7
= [ ]

Task 3
I'm not clever enough to complete the puzzle and find Wizard Whimstaff's secret number. Can you find the total of each set of numbers and then write the answers as words?

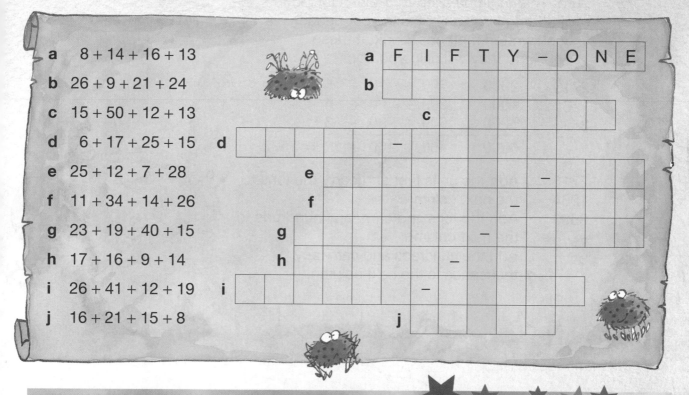

a	8 + 14 + 16 + 13
b	26 + 9 + 21 + 24
c	15 + 50 + 12 + 13
d	6 + 17 + 25 + 15
e	25 + 12 + 7 + 28
f	11 + 34 + 14 + 26
g	23 + 19 + 40 + 15
h	17 + 16 + 9 + 14
i	26 + 41 + 12 + 19
j	16 + 21 + 15 + 8

a F I F T Y – O N E

Sorcerer's Skill Check

These are Mugly and Bugly's favourite revolting recipes. Write the total weight for each of these disgusting dinners.

Slimey Spider Pie
38 g spiders' webs
95 g spiders' legs
65 g murky mud
40 g spiders' eggs
80 g charm powder

Total: _____ g

Shell Crunch
40 g snails (shelled)
34 g slugs
85 g crushed snails' shells
3 g lizards' spit

Total: _____ g

Fly fingers
50 g whole fly wings
18 g ants
52 g freshly squeezed flies
35 g sticky brown paper
50 g fly eggs

Total: _____ g

Grub's up! Give yourself a gold star, but none of our dinner!
Burp!

Written Wizardry

Slurp! This must be a job for Pointy! Instead of **adding large numbers** in your head, use written methods. Look at these and they will help you, too.

```
  2715      2000 +  700 +  10 + 5
  1264      1000 +  200 +  60 + 4
+ 3593      3000 +  500 +  90 + 3
          ──────────────────────────
            6000 + 1400 + 160 + 12 = 7572
```

```
  2715
  1264
+ 3593
───────
  7572
  1 1 1
```

Add the units first and carry the tens to the next column.

Add the tens and carry any hundreds to the next column.

Add the hundreds and carry any thousands to the next column.

Task 1 We need a nap after all this explaining. Can you help us out and write the answers for each of these?

```
a   3 6 2 4          c   1 5 1 9          e   5 9 7 1
  + 1 2 5 8            + 4 6 7 2            +   2 9 9
  ─────────            ─────────            ─────────

        b   2 0 7 4          d   4 3 3 6
          +   6 9 3            + 3 0 8 7
          ─────────            ─────────
```

Task 2 Answer these and you're well on the way to becoming a maths wizard.

```
a   1 2 4 5          c   2 7 3 6          e   1 5 3 2
    5 6 3 5              1 4 5 0              4 0 8 9
  + 1 1 7 6            +   2 3 4          + 2 6 2 3
  ─────────            ─────────          ─────────

        b   3 0 0 8          d     9 2 1
              4 1 9              2 6 6 7
          + 2 9 7 5          + 5 1 8 7
          ─────────          ─────────
```

Task 3 Work your magic and enter the missing number in each clear crystal. Is that crystal clear? Croak! Croak!

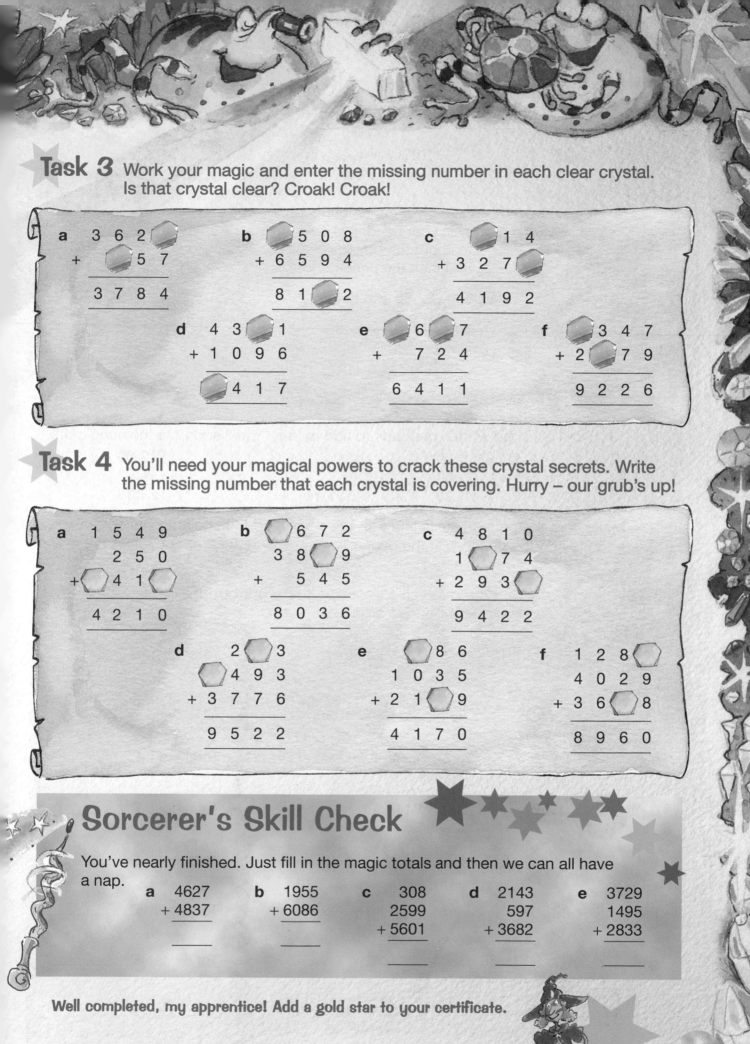

a
```
  3 6 2 ⬡
+   ⬡ 5 7
─────────
  3 7 8 4
```

b
```
  ⬡ 5 0 8
+ 6 5 9 4
─────────
  8 1 ⬡ 2
```

c
```
  ⬡ 1 4
+ 3 2 7 ⬡
─────────
  4 1 9 2
```

d
```
  4 3 ⬡ 1
+ 1 0 9 6
─────────
  ⬡ 4 1 7
```

e
```
  ⬡ 6 ⬡ 7
+   7 2 4
─────────
  6 4 1 1
```

f
```
  ⬡ 3 4 7
+ 2 ⬡ 7 9
─────────
  9 2 2 6
```

Task 4 You'll need your magical powers to crack these crystal secrets. Write the missing number that each crystal is covering. Hurry – our grub's up!

a
```
  1 5 4 9
    2 5 0
+ ⬡ 4 1 ⬡
─────────
  4 2 1 0
```

b
```
  ⬡ 6 7 2
  3 8 ⬡ 9
+   5 4 5
─────────
  8 0 3 6
```

c
```
  4 8 1 0
  1 ⬡ 7 4
+ 2 9 3 ⬡
─────────
  9 4 2 2
```

d
```
    2 ⬡ 3
  ⬡ 4 9 3
+ 3 7 7 6
─────────
  9 5 2 2
```

e
```
  ⬡ 8 6
  1 0 3 5
+ 2 1 ⬡ 9
─────────
  4 1 7 0
```

f
```
  1 2 8 ⬡
  4 0 2 9
+ 3 6 ⬡ 8
─────────
  8 9 6 0
```

Sorcerer's Skill Check

You've nearly finished. Just fill in the magic totals and then we can all have a nap.

a
```
  4627
+ 4837
──────
```

b
```
  1955
+ 6086
──────
```

c
```
   308
  2599
+ 5601
──────
```

d
```
  2143
   597
+ 3682
──────
```

e
```
  3729
  1495
+ 2833
──────
```

Well completed, my apprentice! Add a gold star to your certificate.

Mesmerising Money

When adding **larger amounts of money** in your head, it is easy to count the pounds and then the pence.

What is £12.66 add £14.62?

£12 add £14 is £26.
66p add 62p is £1.28.
The total is £27.28.

You can also use written methods to add money. You'll soon get the hang of it!

£12.66	£10 + £2 + 60p + 6p		£12.66
£14.62	£10 + £4 + 60p + 2p	or	+ £14.62
_____	£20 + £6 + £1.20 + 8p = £27.28		£27.28
			1

Make sure the pounds are in line with the pounds and the pence with the pence.

Add the columns as normal – make sure the correct values are in line.

Task 1

Now you have a try! Use your head to work out the total of each of these broom cupboard bargains.

a £7.12 £4.85 — Total cost: £_____

b £5.41 £5.96 — Total cost: £_____

c £10.73 £8.70 — Total cost: £_____

d £3.99 £11.06 — Total cost: £_____

e £15.24 £11.60 — Total cost: £_____

f £21.37 £8.29 — Total cost: £_____

g £16.50 £21.76 — Total cost: £_____

h £9.03 £16.88 — Total cost: £_____

Task 2

Now use your pen or pencil to work out the tremendous total for each of these.

a £12.99	b £47.80	c £33.64	d £19.56
£25.73	£ 8.88	£17.26	£54.59
_____	_____	_____	_____

Task 3

I've given Mugly and Bugly £30 to spend. Join the pairs of spiders they could buy that total exactly £30.

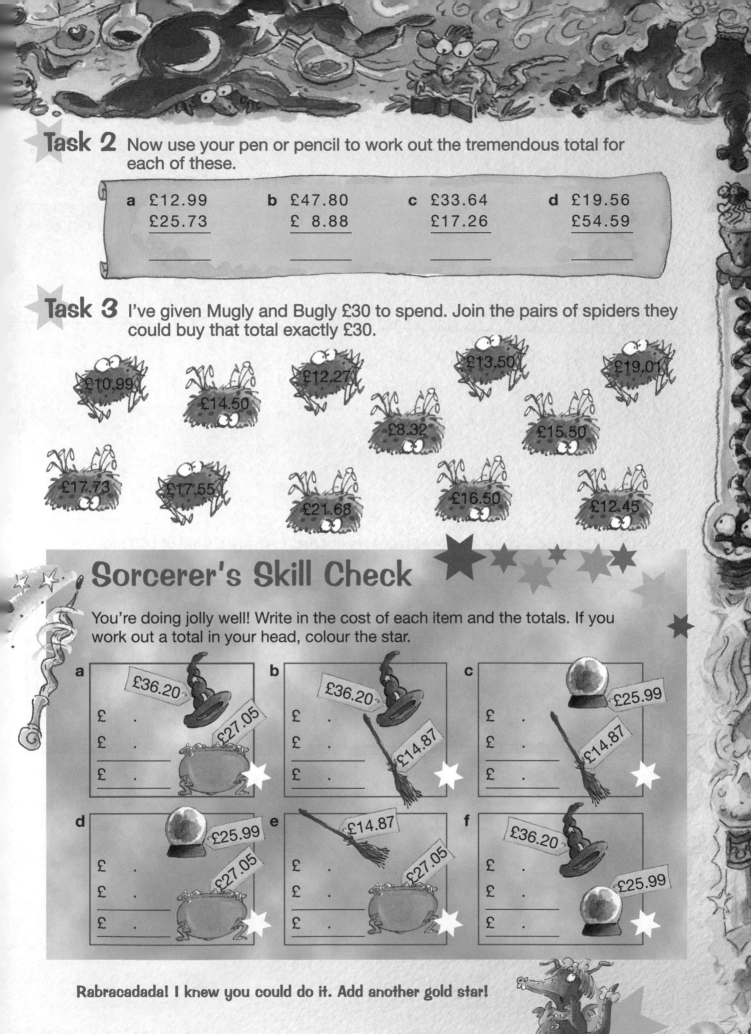

£10.99 £14.50 £12.27 £13.50 £19.01

£8.32 £15.50

£17.73 £17.55 £21.68 £16.50 £12.45

Sorcerer's Skill Check

You're doing jolly well! Write in the cost of each item and the totals. If you work out a total in your head, colour the star.

a
£ .
£ .
£ .
£36.20 £27.05

b
£ .
£ .
£ .
£36.20 £14.87

c
£ .
£ .
£ .
£25.99 £14.87

d
£ .
£ .
£ .
£25.99 £27.05

e
£ .
£ .
£ .
£14.87 £27.05

f
£ .
£ .
£ .
£36.20 £25.99

Rabracadada! I knew you could do it. Add another gold star!

Apprentice Wizard Challenge 1

Challenge 1   Write the answer to each double in this number puzzle.

Across	Down
b 60 + 60	**a** 4000 + 4000
d 230 + 230	**b** 700 + 700
e 8000 + 8000	**c** 130 + 130
g 1400 + 1400	**e** 900 + 900
h 200 + 200	**f** 3000 + 3000
i 7000 + 7000	**g** 120 + 120

Challenge 2   Write how much more is needed to make a total of 6000 for each of these.

a   3000 + _____   **b**   1000 + _____   **c**   2000 + _____

d   5500 + _____   **e**   1200 + _____

f   5900 + _____   **g**   2500 + _____   **h**   700 + _____

i   3100 + _____   **j**   4600 + _____

Challenge 3   Complete these number grids.

a

+	82	105	67	243
33				
150				
49				

b

+	24	91	175	236
68				
112				
307				

Challenge 4 Write the total of each set of numbers.

a

6	32
16	24

Total: _____

b

17	13
65	19

Total: _____

c

37	9
11	22

Total: _____

Challenge 5 Write the answer for each of these.

a
```
  3 5 2 6
+   9 0 5
---------
```

b
```
    7 1 9
  1 3 5 4
+   6 9 3
---------
```

c
```
  2 0 0 4
+ 5 7 9 6
---------
```

d
```
  1 8 9 2
  2 8 0 8
+ 4 1 3 7
---------
```

e
```
  4 1 3 7
  1 5 8 4
+ 2 8 5 9
---------
```

Challenge 6 Find the total of each pair of price tags.

a   £15.60
£27.63   Total Cost = £_____

c   £34.52
£16.79   Total Cost = £_____

b   £22.99
£ 6.04   Total Cost = £_____

d   £19.35
£58.87   Total Cost = £_____

Well done, young apprentice! Another gold star!

Subtraction Sizzlers

Oh dear! Pointy has been trying to tell me that once you know your subtraction bonds, it's easy to **subtract multiples of 10** from other numbers.

Subtractions slip out of my head, though. Oops!

Look at the patterns in this.	Now look at the patterns in this.
8 − 5 = 3	28 − 5 = 23
80 − 50 = 30	280 − 50 = 230
800 − 500 = 300	2800 − 500 = 2300
8000 − 5000 = 3000	28 000 − 5000 = 23 000

Task 1 If you practise with Pointy's patterns, you'll become as clever as him. Then you can help me become a maths wizard too!

a
9 − 4 = ☐
90 − 40 = ☐
900 − 400 = ☐
9000 − 4000 = ☐

b
12 − 6 = ☐
120 − 60 = ☐
1200 − 600 = ☐
12 000 − 6000 = ☐

c
15 − 7 = ☐
150 − 70 = ☐
1500 − 700 = ☐
15 000 − 7000 = ☐

Task 2 Oh dear, I'm still confused! Can you help me?

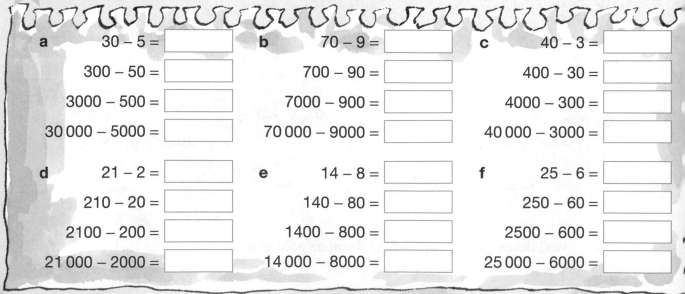

a
30 − 5 = ☐
300 − 50 = ☐
3000 − 500 = ☐
30 000 − 5000 = ☐

b
70 − 9 = ☐
700 − 90 = ☐
7000 − 900 = ☐
70 000 − 9000 = ☐

c
40 − 3 = ☐
400 − 30 = ☐
4000 − 300 = ☐
40 000 − 3000 = ☐

d
21 − 2 = ☐
210 − 20 = ☐
2100 − 200 = ☐
21 000 − 2000 = ☐

e
14 − 8 = ☐
140 − 80 = ☐
1400 − 800 = ☐
14 000 − 8000 = ☐

f
25 − 6 = ☐
250 − 60 = ☐
2500 − 600 = ☐
25 000 − 6000 = ☐

Task 3

This is Wizard Whimstaff's subtraction wand. A number goes in and 40 is subtracted. Can you write the answers in the stars, where the answers come out?

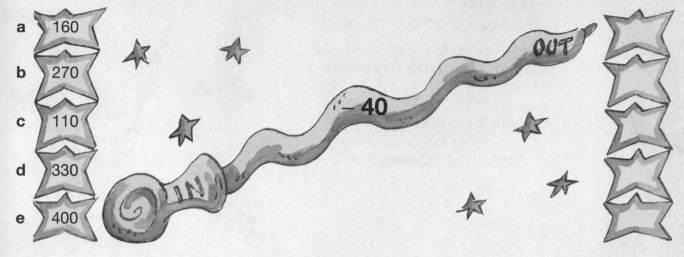

a 160
b 270
c 110
d 330
e 400

$- 40$

Task 4

This subtraction wand takes away 900! Oh dear, my head hurts …

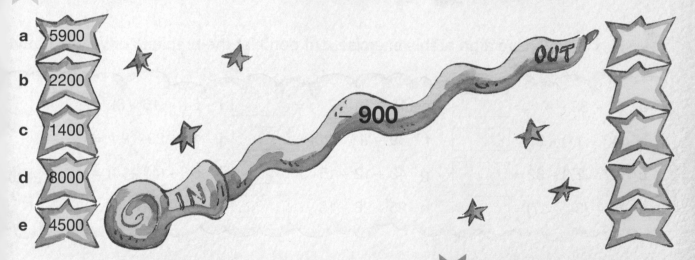

a 5900
b 2200
c 1400
d 8000
e 4500

$- 900$

Sorcerer's Skill Check

Pointy has asked me to do these, but I can't remember how! Can you do them?

a 1900 – 600 = ☐   f 250 – 60 = ☐

b 80 000 – 2000 = ☐   g 320 – 70 = ☐

c 58 000 – 9000 = ☐   h 3100 – 800 = ☐

d 44 000 – 5000 = ☐   i 6000 – 300 = ☐

e 870 – 30 = ☐

Super! Practice has made perfect! Add another gold star to your certificate, young apprentice.

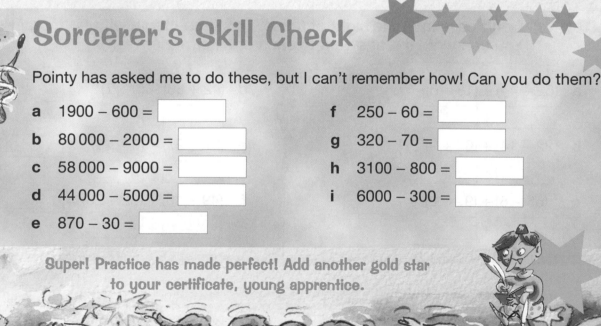

Batty Brackets

Brackets don't have to drive
you batty – just follow the rules!

If there are **no brackets**, work out
the sum **in the order it is written.**

$$34 - 9 + 12 = 37$$

If there are **brackets**, you must
remember to work out the
sum in the brackets first.

$$34 - (9 + 12) = ?$$
$$9 + 12 = 21$$
$$\text{then, } 34 - 21 = 13$$
$$\text{so } 34 - (9 + 12) = 13$$

Task 1   Now have a go at this exercise, but don't let the brackets drive you batty!

a $67 - 32 - 8$ = ☐   **e** $18 + 14 - 7$ = ☐   **i** $54 - (16 + 8)$ = ☐

b $(43 - 11) + 25 =$ ☐   **f** $39 - (43 - 20) =$ ☐   **j** $13 + 23 - 9$ = ☐

c $(17 + 27) - 32 =$ ☐   **g** $43 + 12 + 15$ = ☐   **k** $51 - (43 - 14) =$ ☐

d $62 - (34 + 17) =$ ☐   **h** $25 + 28 - 15$ = ☐   **l** $(19 + 32) - 11 =$ ☐

Task 2 Don't cave in at the sight of these! This time, begin with both brackets.
You can write the answers to each bracket underneath.

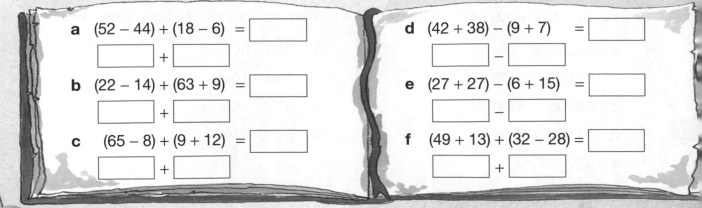

a $(52 - 44) + (18 - 6)$ = ☐
☐ + ☐

b $(22 - 14) + (63 + 9)$ = ☐
☐ + ☐

c $(65 - 8) + (9 + 12)$ = ☐
☐ + ☐

d $(42 + 38) - (9 + 7)$ = ☐
☐ – ☐

e $(27 + 27) - (6 + 15)$ = ☐
☐ – ☐

f $(49 + 13) + (32 - 28)$ = ☐
☐ + ☐

Task 3 Put in the missing brackets to make each answer correct. Just do the best you can.

a 25 − 17 + 6 = 14

25 − 17 + 6 = 2

b 59 − 26 − 15 = 18

59 − 26 − 15 = 48

c 62 − 30 − 22 = 54

62 − 30 − 22 = 10

d 47 − 23 − 12 = 36

47 − 23 − 12 = 12

e 88 − 45 − 14 = 57

88 − 45 − 14 = 29

f 74 − 58 − 15 = 1

74 − 58 − 15 = 31

Task 4 Work out each of these and join them to the correct answer.

a (18 − 14) + (19 − 8) | 10 | **d** (39 − 28) + (4 + 5)

b 42 − (28 + 4) | 15 | **e** (43 − 14) − (29 − 15)

c (46 + 18) − 44 | 20 | **f** (27 + 42) − (38 + 21)

Sorcerer's Skill Check

A vanishing spell has made the + and − signs invisible! You will pass this tantalising test by writing in the missing signs. All the answers must be 25.

a 71 ☐ 23 ☐ 23 = 25

b 37 ☐ 26 ☐ 14 = 25

c (45 ☐ 26) ☐ 6 = 25

d (26 ☐ 9) + (33 ☐ 25) = 25

e 18 ☐ 19 ☐ 12 = 25

f 62 ☐ (21 ☐ 16) = 25

g 17 ☐ (32 ☐ 24) = 25

h (34 + 28) ☐ (14 + 23) = 25

Super sign sorting! It's easy when you know how! Another gold star to add to your certificate! Super!

Dreaded Differences

No need to dread **differences**!
You'll soon get the hang of it!

**What is the difference between
72 and 147?**

To find the **difference between two numbers:**
• start with the smallest number and count on to the next 10
• count on in tens to the nearest whole 10 to the largest number
• count on the units.

(You can also count in hundreds for large numbers.)
The difference is 75 (8 + 60 + 7).

Start with	Count on	to	Count on	to	Count on	to Finish
72	8	80	60	140	7	147

⭐ **Task 1** Use my clever "counting on" method to find the difference between each of these start and finish numbers.

	Start with	Count on	to	Count on	to	Count on	to Finish	Difference
a	47	+		+		+	124	
b	83	+		+		+	116	
c	52	+		+		+	135	
d	129	+		+		+	186	
e	164	+		+		+	203	
f	66	+		+		+	134	
g	78	+		+		+	222	
h	155	+		+		+	245	
i	232	+		+		+	368	

Task 2 This shows some of Wizard Whimstaff's previous apprentices. I have made this chart to show their heights, which includes their hats!

Use my chart to find the difference in height between:

a Hazwiz and Hans

_____ cm

b Harry and Wanda

_____ cm

c Whizzle and Hans

_____ cm

d Wendizle and Hazwiz

_____ cm

e Hans and Harry

_____ cm

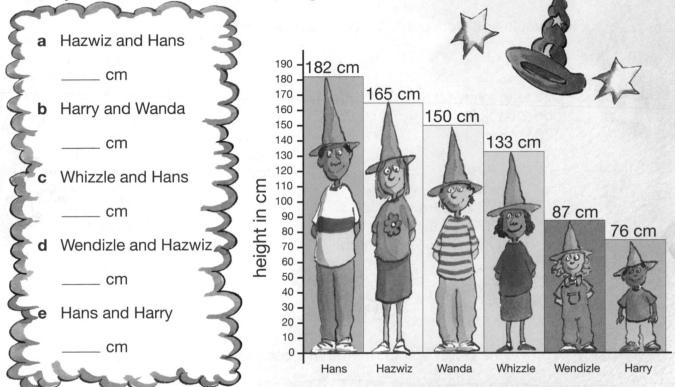

Sorcerer's Skill Check

Mugly and Bugly have been avoiding wizard work and are snoozing under wizard hats. Write the difference for each pair of numbers. Shush, don't wake them up!

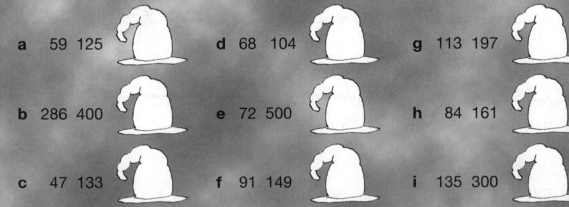

a 59 125

b 286 400

c 47 133

d 68 104

e 72 500

f 91 149

g 113 197

h 84 161

i 135 300

Brain cell alert! Croak, we've been woken to give a gold star to a superstar!

Sublime Subtraction

For **subtracting two numbers** in your head,
here are two **mental methods** to try.

How would you work out 172 flies take away 48 flies?

Grub's up!
172 – 48
172 take away 50 is 122
add 2 back is 124
172 – 48 = 124

Slurp …
172 – 48
172 take away 40 is 132
132 take away 8 is 124
172 – 48 = 124 … burp!

Task 1 Burp! Use our magical mental method for subtracting in your head.

a 156 – 25

b 279 – 63

c 300 – 18

d 568 – 33

e 87 – 39

f 635 – 40

g 103 – 76

h 141 – 99

Task 2 Grub's up! Help us out and fill in the answers to these. We're hungry!

a 310 – 54

b 292 – 19

c 127 – 81

d 184 – 89

e 82 – 27

f 402 – 56

g 119 – 34

h 267 – 89

Task 3 Wizard Whimstaff's cunning code can conjure up tasty food!
Find each answer, then match it to a letter on the code. Slurp!

42	114	67	186	89	125
G	A	E	P	R	L

a 139 – 97 = [ ] _____

145 – 56 = [ ] _____

139 – 25 = [ ] _____

250 – 64 = [ ] _____

156 – 89 = [ ] _____

b 197 – 83 = [ ] _____

262 – 76 = [ ] _____

221 – 35 = [ ] _____

182 – 57 = [ ] _____

150 – 83 = [ ] _____

c 204 – 18 = [ ] _____

118 – 51 = [ ] _____

200 – 86 = [ ] _____

173 – 84 = [ ] _____

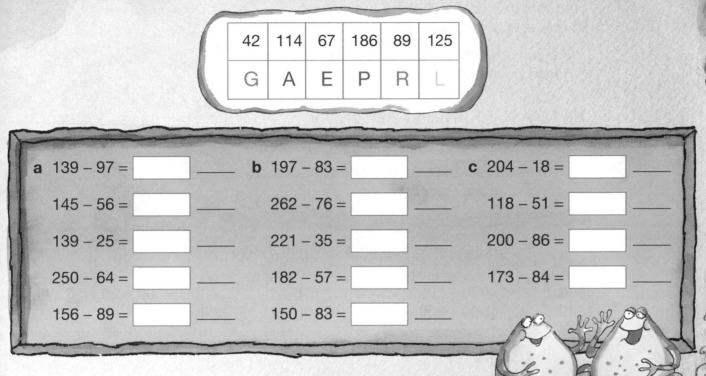

Sorcerer's Skill Check

Cauldrons produce sensational subtraction smoke. See if you can write in the missing magical numbers. Slurp!

a 96

b 132

c 118

d 79

e 207

IN – 56 OUT

f 84

g 325

h 141

i 129

j 237

IN – 78 OUT

I think you should have another gold star! Dabracababra!

Written Wonders

When **subtracting large numbers** that you can't work out in your head, use a wizard and wand written method.

As you are only an apprentice, you have to use pen and paper for now.

$$\begin{array}{r} 4526 \\ -\ 1249 \\ \hline \\ \hline \end{array}$$

$$\begin{array}{r} 4000 + 500 + 20 + 6 \\ -\ 1000 + 200 + 40 + 9 \\ \hline \\ \hline \end{array}$$

Hey Presto! Let's do this one below together.

Change tens to units and hundreds to tens.

$$\begin{array}{r} {}^{1\ 16} \\ 45\cancel{2}\cancel{6} \\ -\ 1249 \\ \hline 7 \end{array}$$

$$\begin{array}{r} 4000 + 500 + 10 + 6 \\ -\ 1000 + 200 + 40 + 9 \\ \hline 7 \end{array}$$

$$\begin{array}{r} {}^{11} \\ {}^{4\ \cancel{1}\ 16} \\ 45\cancel{2}\cancel{6} \\ -\ 1249 \\ \hline 77 \end{array}$$

$$\begin{array}{r} 4000 + 500 + 20 + 16 \\ -\ 1000 + 200 + 40 + 9 \\ \hline 70 + 7 \end{array}$$

$$\begin{array}{r} {}^{11} \\ {}^{4\ \cancel{1}\ 16} \\ 45\cancel{2}\cancel{6} \\ -\ 1249 \\ \hline 3277 \end{array}$$

$$\begin{array}{r} 4000 + 500 + 20 + 16 \\ -\ 1000 + 200 + 40 + 9 \\ \hline 3000 + 200 + 70 + 7 \end{array}$$

You may have to change thousands to hundreds in some questions.

Task 1 Write the answers to these – don't worry if it seems hard at first.

a	694 − 285	b	743 − 356	c	841 − 463	d	704 − 329

Task 2 Write the answers to these – don't worry if it seems hard at first.

a	4738 − 1592	b	9471 − 3803	c	6045 − 2175	d	5962 − 4689
e	7700 − 2935	f	3184 − 1685	g	8256 − 4397	h	9013 − 8416

Task 3 Like an owl, be wise while working out the missing numbers in these.

a
```
  4 7 1 □
- 1 □ 3 8
─────────
  3 0 8 0
```

b
```
  1 8 □ 0
- □ 7 4 5
─────────
    1 4 5
```

c
```
  □ 5 2 3
- 4 7 □ 9
─────────
  1 8 0 4
```

d
```
  8 □ 2 0
-   3 8 4 □
─────────
    4 7 7 9
```

e
```
  9 0 5 □
- 5 4 8 8
─────────
  □ 5 6 9
```

f
```
  7 □ 1 1
- 1 6 1 □
─────────
  5 6 9 9
```

g
```
  □ 6 2 4
- 4 9 □ 3
─────────
    6 9 1
```

h
```
  6 8 0 □
- 2 □ 0 5
─────────
  4 0 9 7
```

Task 4 Here is a tricky problem for you to solve.

Which two numbers with a difference of 250 have a total of 5000?

□ and □

Sorcerer's Skill Check

Use your powerful pen to write perfect answers and you'll soon be a wizard yourself!

a
```
  7384
- 2689
──────
```

b
```
  5104
- 1705
──────
```

c
```
  8269
- 6379
──────
```

d
```
  7452
- 6873
──────
```

It's easy when you know how! Put the gold star on your nearly completed certificate, young apprentice.

Charming Change

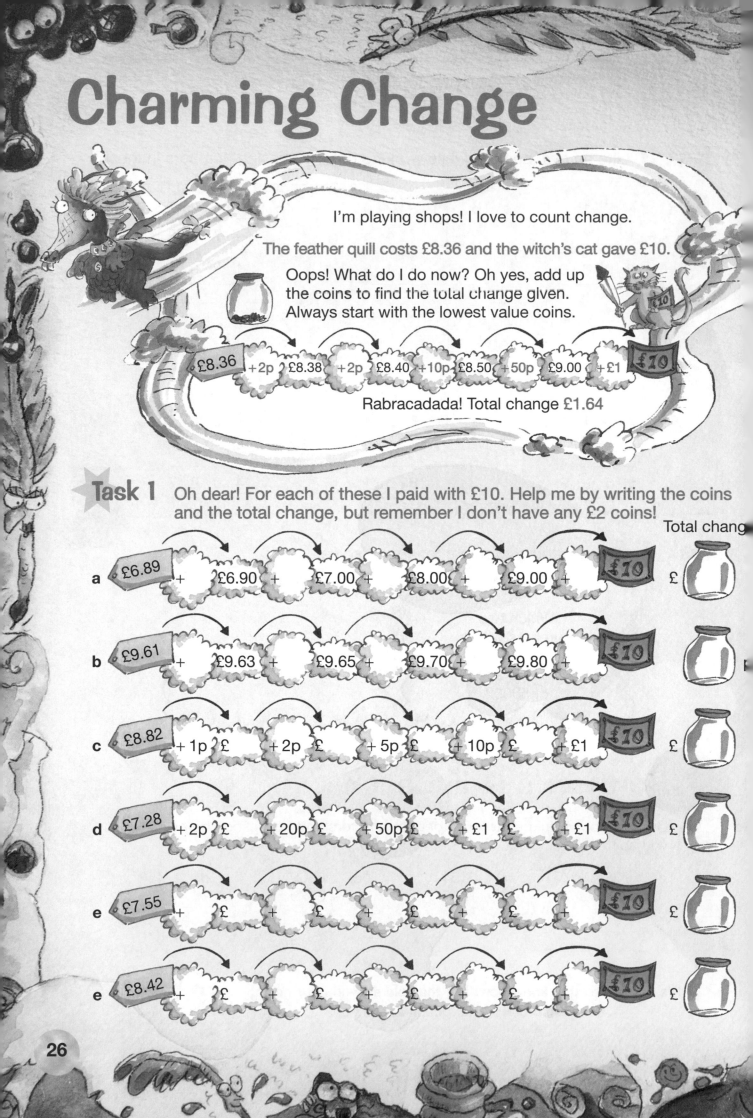

I'm playing shops! I love to count change.

The feather quill costs £8.36 and the witch's cat gave £10.

Oops! What do I do now? Oh yes, add up the coins to find the total change given. Always start with the lowest value coins.

£8.36 +2p £8.38 +2p £8.40 +10p £8.50 +50p £9.00 +£1 £10

Rabracadada! Total change £1.64

Task 1 Oh dear! For each of these I paid with £10. Help me by writing the coins and the total change, but remember I don't have any £2 coins!

Total change

a £6.89 + £6.90 + £7.00 + £8.00 + £9.00 + £10 £

b £9.61 + £9.63 + £9.65 + £9.70 + £9.80 + £10 £

c £8.82 +1p £ +2p £ +5p £ +10p £ +£1 £10 £

d £7.28 +2p £ +20p £ +50p £ +£1 £ +£1 £10 £

e £7.55 + £ + £ + £ + £ + £10 £

e £8.42 + £ + £ + £ + £ + £10 £

26

Task 2 Oh dear! How much change from £5 would I give for each of these?

a £4.10 Change from £5 ____p

b £3.64 Change from £5 £____

c £1.31 Change from £5 £____

d 75p Change from £5 £____

e £2.88 Change from £5 £____

f £0.94 Change from £5 £____

Task 3 Help! I have to work out change from £20! I'm no good with larger sums – can you do it for me?

a £16.99 Change from £20 £____

b £12.04 Change from £20 £____

c £14.56 Change from £20 £____

d £7.80 Change from £20 £____

e £18.27 Change from £20 £____

f £11.49 Change from £20 £____

Sorcerer's Skill Check

Show your change counting skills by completing these.

£1.99 Change from:

£2
a ____p

£5
b ____p

£20
c ____p

£3.36 Change from:

£3.50
d ____p

£5
e ____p

£10
f ____p

Abracadabra! You have done as well as any wizard, place your gold star on your certificate with pride!

Apprentice Wizard Challenge 2

Challenge 1 The answer to these differences have disappeared! Return them to their rightful place by writing in the answers.

a What is the difference between 19 000 m and 2000 m? _____ m

b Subtract 7000 from 29 000. _____

c How much further is 1400 km than 500 km? _____ km

d What is 4100 litres subtract 300 litres? _____ litres

e What is 760 cm take away 80 cm? _____ cm

f How many more is 600 g than 40 g? _____ g

Challenge 2 Some brackets for the brains! Be bold and answer these.

a (57 − 49) + 28 = ☐

b 63 − (42 − 15) = ☐

c (33 + 27) − (16 + 19) = ☐

d (43 − 28) + (17 − 8) = ☐

e 17 + (36 − 11) = ☐

f (78 − 54) + (26 + 9) = ☐

g (19 + 22) − (38 − 15) = ☐

h (34 − 18) − (29 − 17) = ☐

Challenge 3 Enter the differences in the grid to become a fully fledged maths wizard.

a

−	82	67	58
26			
43			
18			

b

−	175	301	119
74			
39			
96			

Challenge 4 Answer the clues to enter the wizard's magic rooms.

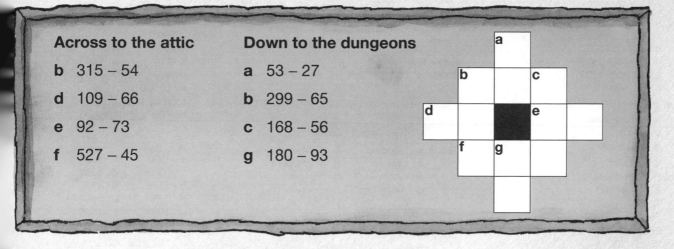

Across to the attic

b 315 – 54

d 109 – 66

e 92 – 73

f 527 – 45

Down to the dungeons

a 53 – 27

b 299 – 65

c 168 – 56

g 180 – 93

Challenge 5 Transform these take aways into amazing answers.

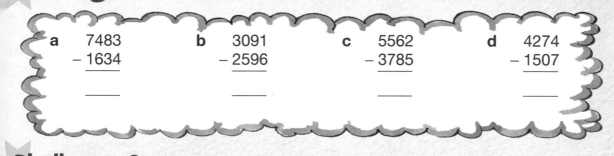

a   7483
   – 1634
   _____

b   3091
   – 2596
   _____

c   5562
   – 3785
   _____

d   4274
   – 1507
   _____

Challenge 6 Use your change conjuring skills to calculate the answers to these.

a £5   Change: £____   £1.63

b £1   Change: ____p   18p

c £10   Change: £____   £8.06

d   Change: ____p   £7.49

e £20   Change: £____   £12.34

f £5   Change: £____   £0.77

Slurp! You've got your last gold star!

Answers

Pages 2–3

Task 1 **a** 12 120 1200 12 000
       b 16 160 1600 16 000
       c 10 100 1000 10 000

Task 2 **a** 22 220 2200
       b 50 500 5000
       c 32 320 3200
       d 28 280 2800
       e 48 480 4800
       f 64 640 6400

Task 3 **a** 360 g
       b 420 eyeballs
       c 900 g
       d 240 spiders
       e 3000 ml

Sorcerer's Skill Check
     2100 → 4200
     7000 → 14 000
     5000 → 10 000
     280 → 560
     350 → 700
     1600 → 3200

Pages 4–5

Task 1 **a** 100 200 300
       b 500 300 100
       c 300 200 400

Task 2 **a** 200   **d** 250
       b 100   **e** 20
       c 50   **f** 390

Task 3 500 → 500
        700 → 300
        270 → 730
        400 → 600
        460 → 540
        290 → 710

Task 4 **a** 3000   **e** 1000
       b 2000   **f** 5000
       c 100   **g** 1800
       d 4300   **h** 2400

Sorcerer's Skill Check
    a 300
    b 50
    c any pair totalling 600
    d 2200
    e 1500
    f any pair totalling 3000

Pages 6–7

Task 1 **a** 385   **e** 853
       b 359   **f** 238
       c 664   **g** 843
       d 466   **h** 521

Task 2 **a** 310   **c** 772
       b 750   **d** 753

Task 3 **a** 602 I   **c** 374 F
         926 T   602 I
         483 A   790 N
         161 L   161 L
         237 Y   483 A
                  790 N
       b 855 S   546 D
         519 P
         483 A
         602 I
         790 N

Sorcerer's Skill Check
    a   157   **d**   154
        86   71   71   83
    b   304   **e**   222
      147   157   139   83
    c   123   **f**   283
       44   79   129   154

Pages 8–9

Task 1 **a** 65   **c** 47
       b 124   **d** 55

Task 2 **a** 69   **d** 78
       b 120   **e** 111
       c 102   **f** 65

Task 3 **a** fifty-one   **f** eighty-five
       b eighty   **g** ninety-seven
       c ninety   **h** fifty-six
       d sixty-three   **i** ninety-eight
       e seventy-two   **j** sixty
       Secret number: THIRTY-SIX

Sorcerer's Skill Check
     318 g   162 g   205 g

Pages 10 –11

Task 1 **a** 4882   **d** 7423
       b 2767   **e** 6270
       c 6191

Task 2 **a** 8056   **d** 8775
       b 6402   **e** 8244
       c 4420

Task 3 **a** 3627   **d** 4321
          157   5417
       b 1508   **e** 5687
         8102   **f** 6347
       c 914   2879
         3278

Task 4 **a** 2411   **d** 253
       b 3672   5493
         3819   **e** 986
       c 1674   2149
         2938   **f** 1283
                  3648

Sorcerer's Skill Check
    a 9464   **d** 6422
    b 8041   **e** 8057
    c 8508

Pages 12–13

Task 1 **a** £11.97   **e** £26.84
       b £11.37   **f** £29.66
       c £19.43   **g** £38.26
       d £15.05   **h** £25.91

Task 2 **a** £38.72   **c** £50.90
       b £56.68   **d** £74.15

Task 3 £10.99 + £19.01
        £21.68 + £8.32
        £12.45 + £17.55
        £13.50 + £16.50
        £14.50 + £15.50
        £17.73 + £12.27

Sorcerer's Skill Check
    a £63.25   **d** £53.04
    b £51.07   **e** £41.92
    c £40.86   **f** £62.19

Pages 14–15

Challenge 1

	Across	Down
b	120	**a** 8000
d	460	**b** 1400
e	16 000	**c** 260
g	2800	**e** 1800
h	400	**f** 6000
i	14 000	**g** 240

Challenge 2
    a 3000   **f** 100
    b 5000   **g** 3500
    c 4000   **h** 5300
    d 500   **i** 2900
    e 4800   **j** 1400

Challenge 3
    a 115 138 100 276
       232 255 217 393
       131 154 116 292
    b 92 159 243 304
       136 203 287 348
       331 398 482 543

Challenge 4
    a 78 **b** 114 **c** 79

Challenge 5
    a 4431   **d** 8837
    b 2766   **e** 8580
    c 7800

Challenge 6
    a £43.23   **c** £51.31
    b £29.03   **d** £78.22

Pages 16–17

Task 1 **a** 5 50 500 5000
       b 6 60 600 6000
       c 8 80 800 8000

Task 2 **a** 25 250 2500 25 000
       b 61 610 6100 61 000
       c 37 370 3700 37 000
       d 19 190 1900 19 000
       e 6 60 600 6000
       f 19 190 1900 19 000

Task 3 **a** 120   **d** 290
       b 230   **e** 360
       c 70

Task 4 **a** 5000   **d** 7100
       b 1300   **e** 3600
       c 500

Sorcerer's Skill Check
    a 1300   **f** 190
    b 78 000   **g** 250
    c 49 000   **h** 2300
    d 39 000   **i** 5700
    e 840

Pages 18–19

Task 1
a 27 g 70
b 57 h 38
c 12 i 30
d 11 j 27
e 25 k 22
f 16 l 40

Task 2
a 8 + 12 = 20
b 8 + 72 = 80
c 57 + 21 = 78
d 80 − 16 = 64
e 54 − 21 = 33
f 62 + 4 = 66

Task 3
a (25 − 17) + 6 = 14
  25 − (17 + 6) = 2
b (59 − 26) − 15 = 18
  59 − (26 − 15) = 48
c 62 − (30 − 22) = 54
  (62 − 30) − 22 = 10
d 47 − (23 − 12) = 36
  (47 − 23) − 12 = 12
e 88 − (45 − 14) = 57
  (88 − 45) − 14 = 29
f (74 − 58) − 15 = 1
  74 − (58 − 15) = 31

Task 4
a (18 − 14) + (19 − 8) = 15
b 42 − (28 + 4) = 10
c (46 + 18) − 44 = 20
d (39 − 28) + (4 + 5) = 20
e (43 − 14) − (29 − 15) = 15
f (27 + 42) − (38 + 21) = 10

Sorcerer's Skill Check
a 71 − 23 − 23 = 25
b 37 − 26 + 14 = 25
c (45 − 26) + 6 = 25
d (26 − 9) + (33 − 25) = 25
e 18 + 19 − 12 = 25
f 62 − (21 + 16) = 25
g 17 + (32 − 24) = 25
h (34 + 28) − (14 + 23) = 25

Pages 20–21

Task 1
a 77 f 68
b 33 g 144
c 83 h 90
d 57 i 136
e 39

Task 2
a 17 cm d 78 cm
b 74 cm e 106 cm
c 49 cm

Sorcerer's Skill Check
a 66 f 58
b 114 g 84
c 86 h 77
d 36 i 165
e 428

Pages 22–23

Task 1
a 131 e 48
b 216 f 595
c 282 g 27
d 535 h 42

Task 2
a 256 e 55
b 273 f 346
c 46   g 85
d 95   h 178

Task 3
a 42 G   c 186 P
  89 R   67 E
  114 A   114 A
  186 P   89   R
  67 E

b 114 A
  186 P
  186 P
  125 L
  67   E

Sorcerer's Skill Check
a 40   f 6
b 76   g 247
c 62   h 63
d 23   i 51
e 151 j 159

Pages 24–25

Task 1
a 409 c 378
b 387 d 375

Task 2
a 3146 e 4765
b 5668 f 1499
c 3870 g 3859
d 1273 h 597

Task 3
a 4718 e 9057
  1638   3569
b 1890 f 7311
  1745   1612
c 6523 g 5624
  4719   4933
d 8620 h 6802
  3841   2705

Task 4 2625 and 2375

Sorcerer's Skill Check
a 4695 c 1890
b 3399 d 579

Pages 26–27

Task 1
a £3.11 d £2.72
b 39p   e £2.45
c £1.18 f £1.58

Task 2
a 90p   d £4.25
b £1.36 e £2.12
c £3.69 f £4.06

Task 3
a £3.01 d £12.20
b £7.96 e £1.73
c £5.44 f £8.51

Sorcerer's Skill Check
a 1p   d 14p
b £3.01 e £1.64
c £18.01 f £6.64

Pages 28–29

Challenge 1
a 17 000 m d 3800 litres
b 22 000   e 680 cm
c 900 km   f 560 g

Challenge 2
a 36 e 42
b 36 f 59
c 25 g 18
d 24 h 4

Challenge 3
a 56 41 32
   39 24 15
   64 49 40
b 101 227 45
   136 262 80
   79 205 23

Challenge 4

	Across		Down
b	261	a	26
d	43	b	234
e	19	c	112
f	482	g	87

Challenge 5
a 5849 c 1777
b 495   d 2767

Challenge 6
a £3.37 d 51p
b 82p   e £7.66
c £1.94 f £4.23

Wizard's Certificate of Excellence

★ **Devilish Doubles**

★ **Subtraction Sizzlers**

★ **Troublesome Totals**

★ **Batty Brackets**

★ **Mental Meddling**

★ **Dreaded Differences**

★ **Awesome Adding**

★ **Sublime Subtraction**

★ **Written Wizardry**

★ **Written Wonders**

★ **Mesmerising Money**

★ **Charming Change**

★ **Apprentice Wizard Challenge 1**

★ **Apprentice Wizard Challenge 2**

This is to state that Wizard Whimstaff awards

Apprentice _____

the title of Maths Wizard. Congratulations!

Published 2002
Revised edition 2007

Letts Educational
4 Grosvenor Place, London SW1X 7DL
School enquiries: 01539 564910
Parent & student enquiries: 01539 564913
E-mail: mail@lettsed.co.uk   Website: www.letts-educational.com

Text, design and illustrations © Letts Educational Ltd 2002

Author: Paul Broadbent
Book Concept and Development:
Helen Jacobs, Publishing Director; Sophie London, Project Editor
Design and Editorial: Cambridge Publishing Management Ltd.
Illustrations: Mike Phillips and Neil Chapman (Beehive Illustration)
Cover Illustration: Neil Chapman
Cover Design: Linda Males

British Library Cataloguing in Publication Data

A CIP record for this book is available from the British Library.

ISBN 978 1 84315 095 4

Printed in Italy

Colour reproduction by PDQ Digital Media Solutions Ltd, Bungay, Suffo